CLOUDS

by Mary Meinking

Cody Koala

An Imprint of Pop!
popbooksonline.com

abdopublishing.com
Published by Pop!, a division of ABDO, PO Box 398166, Minneapolis,
Minnesota 55439. Copyright © 2019 by POP, LLC. International copyrights
reserved in all countries. No part of this book may be reproduced in any
form without written permission from the publisher. Pop!™ is a trademark
and logo of POP, LLC.

Printed in the United States of America, North Mankato, Minnesota

042018
092018

**THIS BOOK CONTAINS
RECYCLED MATERIALS**

Distributed in paperback by North Star Editions, Inc.

Cover Photo: Shutterstock Images
Interior Photo: Shutterstock Images, 1, 5 (top), 5 (bottom right), 9, 13 (top
middle), 19, 21; iStockphoto, 5 (bottom left), 6–7, 10, 13 (bottom left), 15;
David R. Frazier/Science Source, 13 (bottom right); NASA/JPL, 16

Editor: Meg Gaertner
Series Designer: Laura Mitchell

Library of Congress Control Number: 2017963472

Publisher's Cataloging-in-Publication Data

Names: Meinking, Mary, author.
Title: Clouds / by Mary Meinking.
Description: Minneapolis, Minnesota : Pop!, 2019. | Series: Weather watch |
    Includes online resources and index.
Identifiers: ISBN 9781532160523 (lib.bdg.) | ISBN 9781635178401 (pbk) | ISBN
    9781532161643 (ebook) |
Subjects: LCSH: Clouds--Juvenile literature. | Weather--Juvenile literature.
    |Meteorology--Juvenile literature.
Classification: DDC 551.5--dc23

Hello! My name is

Cody Koala

Pop open this book and you'll find QR codes like this one, loaded with information, so you can learn even more!

Scan this code* and others like it while you read,

or visit the website below to make this book pop.

popbooksonline.com/clouds

*Scanning QR codes requires a web-enabled smart device with a QR code reader app and a camera.

Table of Contents

Chapter 1

What Are Clouds?

Water vapor rises high in the sky. It cools and forms water drops. The drops stick to floating dust. Some turn into ice. When many drops come together, they form a cloud.

Watch a video here!

No two clouds are alike.

Clouds come in different

shapes, sizes, and colors.

The wind, temperature, and amount of water make each cloud unique.

Clouds look white because their water drops reflect sunlight.

Chapter 2

Types of Clouds

Cirrus clouds are made of ice crystals. The wind blows them to look like a horse's tail. They are high up in the sky. They usually mean fair weather.

Learn more here!

Cumulus clouds are puffy like cotton balls. They form on warm summer days. Cumulus clouds are a sign of nice weather.

An average cumulus cloud weighs as much as 100 elephants.

Stratus clouds are gray clouds that cover the sky like a blanket. They may bring light rain or mist. Fog is a type of stratus cloud that comes very low to the ground.

Cirrus

above 18,000 ft
(5,500 m)

Cumulus

below 6,000 ft
(1,800 m)

Cloud Types

Stratus

below 6,000 ft
(1,800 m)

On the Job

Clouds are important because they cool and heat Earth. On hot days, clouds block the sunlight. They keep the ground cool.

Learn more here!

At night, clouds act like a blanket. They keep the ground warm. Clouds trap Earth's heat. They keep heat from leaving the **atmosphere**.

Read the Clouds

Since ancient times, farmers and sailors have used clouds to **predict** the weather. Different types of clouds bring different types of weather.

Complete an activity here!

Relax in the grass to watch puffy cumulus clouds. Grab an umbrella when there are gray stratus clouds. All clouds tell a story. Just look up!

Making Connections

Text-to-Self

How do the different types of clouds affect your daily life?

Text-to-Text

Have you read other books about clouds? What new information did you learn?

Text-to-World

Do people still "read" the clouds? Why is it important to know about clouds?

Glossary

atmosphere – the layer of gas that surrounds Earth and separates it from space.

cirrus – a wispy type of cloud that forms high in the sky.

cumulus – a thick type of cloud that has a fluffy shape.

predict – to say something that might happen in the future.

stratus – a low type of cloud that stretches over most of the sky.

water vapor – water in the form of a gas.

Index

Online Resources

popbooksonline.com

Thanks for reading this Cody Koala book!

Scan this code* and others like it in this book, or visit the website below to make this book pop!

popbooksonline.com/clouds

*Scanning QR codes requires a web-enabled smart device with a QR code reader app and a camera.